LIGHT PERSISTS

Light Persists

Poems by

Jane Ellen Glasser

UNIVERSITY OF TAMPA PRESS • TAMPA, FLORIDA

The photograph on the cover was taken in Alarcon, Spain, by photographer Lance
Lavenstein and produced as a poster dedicated to Amnesty International in memory of
Jessica R. Glasser and John Kelsey. Copyright © 2006 by Lance Lavenstein.

Manufactured in the United States of America
Printed on acid-free paper ∞
First Edition

The University of Tampa Press
401 West Kennedy Boulevard
Tampa, FL 33606

ISBN-10 1-59732-004-8 • ISBN-13: 978-1-59732-003-0 (hbk.)
ISBN-10 1-59732-005-6 • ISBN-13: 978-1-59732-005-4 (pbk.)

Browse & order online at

http://utpress.ut.edu

Library of Congress Cataloging-in-Publication Data

Glasser, Jane Ellen, 1944-
  Light persists : poems / by Jane Ellen Glasser.-- 1st ed.
     p. cm.
   ISBN-10: 1-59732-004-8 (hbk : alk. paper) ISBN-10: 1-59732-005-6 (pbk : alk. paper)
   ISBN-13: 978-1-59732-003-0 (hbk : alk. paper) ISBN-13: 978-1-59732-005-4 (pbk. : alk. paper)
   I. Title.
   PS3607.L3735L54 2006
   811'.6--dc22   2006002792

Contents

I

II

III

In the midst of darkness, light persists.

– Gandhi

In loving memory of my daughter Jessica
May 18, 1974—May 24, 1996

I

The Cormorant

Have you known him—
the one who seams
the elements in his wake?

The sky falls
on his head,
there is fire
in his eyes,
the river opens
and closes
on his neck.

Have you known
the falling
which is not
falling
but the head
dreaming down
through darkness
to the place
of the body?

Have you known
the pull
of the bottom
and the silver
of the bottom
and the black mud
of the bottom
and the ache
of the one
who stays gone
so long

the waves
erase him?

And have you felt
the light
reach down
to claim you—
and did you rise
like a charmed snake
somewhere else?

Earley Farm Road

—Sweet Briar, Virginia

Laboring up a road
that went from black to clay,
I passed the quiet fields
where cows graze.

The road became a cut.
On either side, my eyes
kept going, leaping
into shadow.

And then the woods
stopped, the hills fell off
around me. I stood
in an openness,

stunned still
in a sky-swept place
where time and the world
dropped away

until I was nothing
but joy, the joy
of something small
loosening into space.

I would have stayed
and built a house
inside that stalled pitch
but I had known

other times like this—
at the ocean's edge,
on a mountain
wrapped in stars,

or, once, in the dark
cathedral of a foreign city
where I lived
and could not live.

Another Time

I was delivering my daughter
to college. Everything
eighteen years can gather
was the dragging weight

of the U-Haul. For ten hours
she slept, curled
away from me, her buttocks
up against the shaft.

Was she gearing up for some
reckless future? What was
I thinking! Along the way
there are places

that beckon us to stop, or warn—
last chance! When I knew
my mother was dying,
when I saw her shriveling

around a hardness
that ached to be revealed,
we talked about everything
unimportant. It was easy—

two routes falling
west and south to empty out
in Atlanta. The next day
I moved her in. I did what

mothers do. It was work.
Hard work. Sometimes
the body is the only
way we have.

In Dreams

the man I divorced a lifetime ago
keeps coming back like letters
addressed to an abandoned house.

Sometimes we argue
(as we did in our shared life),
a desperate volley of guilt
and blame. Only now
I fix the odds in my favor.
How sweet the slammed
delivery of released anger!

Other nights he shows up
with those sad beseeching eyes
of a dog who knows he's done
something wrong, terribly wrong
(although he's not sure what).

Naturally, I forgive him
(as I didn't in our shared life)
and even though he's newly, happily
married (for the third time),
he confesses he loves me still,
loves me best (in the way all firsts
inherit the biggest rooms in our heart);

and then we fall toward each other
like adjacent walls collapsing inward.

It's so beautifully tragic,
those nights when we stand there
crying, holding on to each other,
knowing (as we did in our shared life)
that no one can live in that ruin.

Inheritance

I never saw you kiss another
unless a dry quill scratched
across paper counts.

I never saw your eyes light
upon a body the way early sun
fingers and reveals the land.

I didn't understand a love
that wasn't love but need
fashioned from the need

not to be known. You said once,
in a harsh, confiding tone,
A woman is a hole in the bed—

that's all, as if the moon
were a punched out place
any launching could penetrate.

And though I ached to believe
your wisdom wrong, Mother,
for too many years I was

a faceless bride of emptiness,
a grave for the tossed
soil and stones of your lesson.

A Felled Statue in the Underbrush at the Parking Lot

How long had he lain there,
one leg crushed, one foot
missing? Leaves nested
where his raised dirty knees

made a hollow. What use
the little bird of his penis,
the arrows still in the quiver,
his wings pinned under him?

Just a boy now lying naked
in the grass on a summer day
dreaming up at the heavens,
that great height from which

Icarus fell to teach us a lesson.
Did anyone stop to notice
Cupid tumbling from the sky?
What myth will we make

when afterwards, half-buried
in the underbrush, love's accident
surprises us, stares up at us
out of our crippled lives?

The Open Door

His waking hours love a window.
He quickens to any action—
trajectory of wings,
free-sailing leaf, or beast
nosing the bushes in the yard.

His senses tell him there is something
so much bigger than his life
waiting for him on the other side.

Today, marvelous accident,
the door has been left open!

Again, and again, he launches
one paw into the cold light.

Memorial

She left her clothes
folded at the foot of her bed.
She had shaved her head
earlier that morning and left
her hair by an open window
for birds to soften
their nests. She left
her money and her keys
and her name in her purse
on a counter top.
Just like that—
she walked out
of her house
and out of town
and she would have kept walking,
pushed along by a gentle hand,
but the wind had other plans.

When she came to a wall
of earth-colored rock,
there was no going over or around,
and she was tired,
relieved to be stopped.
She stood before the rock face—
as many times she had stood
naked before mirrors
or the appraising eyes of men—
and gave herself over
to the cool reflection
of all she would become.

II

The Parrot-Ox

The parrot-ox
is clearly confused,
as evidently
so were his parents.

Being both heavy and light,
he can neither
fly nor root,
which makes his life

a kind of hovering
between two things
that cross each other out.
All play is work,

all drudgery is sport,
and so he spends his days
busily doing nothing,
circling square

fields of thought
like a practical idealist.
At night he holds forth
in a neighborhood bar

in his undertaker's suit
and Indian headdress.
He drinks to sober up
and tell again

the sad joke
of how we die at birth

into opposites.
And then he laughs

till he cries and cries
till he laughs,
sorrow and joy
mixing it up in his blood.

Six Ways to Hide

Eat yourself
into a greatcoat
of sleepy flesh.
Who would think
to look for you
inside yourself?

Be porcupine-ish.
Wake to write
dour lines in the dark.
No one will bother you

in a penthouse
with a broken elevator
or on a perch on Everest.
Fly off

to an early retirement.
Hurl spit, shake
yourself hard
and shoot back
like a bad monkey.

Lose yourself
in a fifth.

Or be as genteel
as the chameleon.
Nod and smile
from the leaf of a chair;
agree to disappear.

The Age of Animals

Elephants are born
gray, wrinkled,
loose strands
fringing the moth-
bitten ears and crown.
For as long as they
live, they are old.

Others gray first
inside, a secret
that leaks out
in a dog's muzzle.

Cats swell and root.
Like beans in a bag,
all their years
sink to the bottom.

On the sea's floor
where starfish drown
their losses,
each new spoke
is a child, each star,
a wheel of ages.

To go backwards,
snakes drop shadows
in woods where birds
never lose teeth,
memories, their looks.

For one hundred years
whatever changes inside
their vaulted shells, turtles
keep to themselves.

Dog Days

They knew it was Sirius,
those ancients who sat
stuporous in their sticky sheets,
too zapped to peel a grape

but not to kick the dog.
Someone had to take the rap,
and so they hurled their curses
at the heavens, only backwards:

Mad dog! they cried, aiming
for the mutt at Helios's feet,
not daring to incur the real heat
of the big dogs, the Olympians,

who also sat, lolling
on their soggy clouds,
too whipped to fight or cheat
or meddle in men's folly.

Complaint to Aphrodite

What in the name of the gods were you thinking
to let your golden-haired boy go streaking
on a snow-swept February day?
Dressed in nothing but a quiver,
couldn't you foresee he'd shiver
himself into a nasty cold? What way
is that to mother your son—a boy
flighty and given to mischief! For toys,
I know boys like to play with weapons
but why not rubber darts or water guns
instead of stinging arrows? Admit it,
he's a sociopath in the making, a misfit,
a literal pain in the ass! Okay, it's true
he'd never be the death of you
and that hoity-toity bunch on Mount Olympus,
but have a heart, take pity on the rest of us.
Talk to your son; don't let him think he's above
all moral law. For starters, you can exhort
the little brat not to sport
with any game as dangerous as love!

At the End of Down

When the father was first a father
he was a god; he lived
in the biggest house in the sky.

Then he came down a little.
Then he was a bird and life moved
under the shadow of his wing.

One day he put on his shadow,
a dark hairy suit, and beat
his chest till the earth trembled

and opened up and ate him.
Then he learned to crawl
and live in a house of dirt

where he was safe;
there was nowhere left to fall
in the daughter's heart.

The Moronic Ox: A Fable

Because he hated the brand
of the sun on his back
and having dirt on his feet
even on Sundays
and found a life
braced to a groaning weight
was getting him nowhere

and because he dreamed of seas
of grass and the pool
of a shade tree
where he could lose himself
in the anywhere of song

when he refused to work the fields
the villagers called him
weak in the head,
a good-for-nothing
who would set
a dangerous example

so they tried him
and found him guilty
of plotting to overthrow
what their bones knew—
that life is its own burden,
a blind pulling from birth to death—

and then they turned him
on a spit and feasted
and carried him
in their bellies to the fields.

That Kind

I am that kind of dog. I stand out
in the storm and raise
the rod of my tail and wait.

Can't you see me? I am alone,
like you. Like you,
I am black against the black.

I am untouched and untouchable.
Your truest son. Send me a sign.
Send it down on my dog's head.

Not this. Not the hands
of the rain along my back. Not this
spilling dish. Don't you know

what kind of dog I am? Show me
your bared teeth! The white heat
of your cracking whip! O Merciful.

Mechanically Speaking

If you were born a machine
and stayed a machine,
that was your life
and you accepted it.

No, after a time
you willed it so.
There were those who
treated you like a somebody,

and one who would have
loved you. You claimed
you weren't built for that—
no heart or brain,

no mouth to speak of—
and blamed the Company
for the company you couldn't
keep. I know better.

I've known a toaster
to unplug itself and fly off,
a Singer to put on a dress
it seamed and dance away;

and once a man
who hid his face behind
his hands became a clock.
And he was happy as a clock.

Meditation on Rain
The answering machine speaks

It's raining today.
I have never seen the rain
or felt the rain

but I can hear it
at the window
and I know that it is

possible to love
something for its sound.
I don't think

the heart is a heart.
I think it is an ear
or a plastic cup.

And the rain—why
the rain could be
anything

that falls
and keeps falling into us
with an urgent voice.

After I Became a Poet

The answering machine speaks

After I became a poet
and spoke in poems
I noticed the world

pulling away.
Some hung up
on a first line.

Some listened and left
no hellos, no good-byes,
as if something I said

offended them. Even
my friends the poets
(preferring to read

themselves) stopped
calling. And then
when I was sad

and missed the world
and thought to call
it up in prose,

out of that good quiet
house of loneliness
came poems.

Flatware

Spoon
    So much
    has washed over me,
    licked me clean
    till I arch
    like the bony
    dome of a mouth.
    My cupped heart
    keeps spilling
    into a dark
    that has teeth.
    In my place
    beside the knife
    I swallow grief.

Knife
    When I was young
    I was harmless
    as a child's finger.
    Whatever I touched
    I smeared. Then
    I grew taller,
    bolder, my body
    sharpened against
    its own kind.
    Now anything
    tough I can handle.
    Flesh is flesh.

Fork
    Take my advice.
    Let things fall
    through your fingers.
    They'll show you
    what counts.

No need to point
or raise a fist,
and you can't wring
sorrow from one
hand. Hold
yourself straight
but be of four minds
like the wind.

III

The Wait

Where one world ends
and another begins
she sits, as all waiting sits,
on an edge.

Wrapped in her wings,
she has planted herself
on an apron of grass
at the bulkhead's rim—

a starting line of sorts.
To cross is to fall or fly,
claim water or air
over her squatter's portion.

Rain falls. Hours and weeks fall.
The tide comes in and goes out
like hunger.
She won't be moved.

Nearby, day and night
nearby, her loosely
anchored mate shuttles
between the banks of her vision.

Naturally, she pretends
not to see him, to be so
caught up in her own doing,
which to the eye is nothing,

but you *know*, you *feel* her
pouring her heat down

evenly as the sun on creation
as her neck and head

throw a black question
mark into the river
where, like all questions,
despite its weight it floats.

A Woman Leans

Framed in the doorway,
stalled between out and in,
a woman leans
the way a broom angles
against a wall on church Sundays.

The day is heating up,
heavy with haze.
Now and then
a shape or a sound swims by.

Where are the boys
who own the streets?

Where are the old ones
who would root
like potted plants on their porches?

Don't ask after the men!

Let children fend for themselves,
the stove sleep,
and human dogs scavenge:

there will be no work done today.

Halcyon

You imagine a woman
turning off lights,
putting each room
to bed. Sleep,
she whispers,
as she rocks you
in a black felt sky.
Toes, fingers, thoughts
swim off,
blind fish
in a stream
sunk so deep
when your dreams
call to you
like children
you are dead
to their cries.

What Are They Doing in There When I'm Not Sleeping?

I imagine a gypsy camp, spangles of sunlight
falling on trailers, tents. They work the night shift
so they should be sleeping. Yet sometimes
I feel them there, behind peepholes.

Are they plotting? Concocting scenarios
or rehearsing on a set? It's a company
whose membership keeps changing
into the trunked guises of a small town circus.

Perhaps they're moving, packing or unpacking
whatever tonight's illusion might require:
pigeons, bouquets and brilliant scarves
to pull from their hats and sleeves;

knives that take shape around a woman.
Maybe, like crimes of passion, their acts
are all impromptu. They can't get life
or death for what they do

and there's no catching them. Like stars
in the white-out of morning, their caravans
vanish when I wake in my singular self
and I think I know what I'm doing.

Carrying

I want to carry you
inside me,
a ruler's length;
to measure my step
by your weight;
to keep walking
into my life
each moment
with the delicacy and care
of knowing I am
a trustee,
a treasure house,
a museum of possibility.

Such radiance!
strangers exclaim,
softening at the sight
of mystery.

In this way
you feed me,
fill me,
expand me
at my core.

When I place my hand there,
just so,
I can feel you
moving like a lover
to meet me.

Who can say
I have not yet
something
to give to the world!

Breasts

So much variety:
whipped egg-whites
with dark peaks,
dangling crocheted purses
grandmothers carry,
melons—like a display
in a restaurant window—
that never spoil.

Like Goldilocks, we try them—
big, medium, small—
and if we're lucky
we're satisfied with our portion.

Only glands and fat,
we tell ourselves,
yet in mammograms
held sideways they look,
as they must to boys,
like sundaes topped with cherries.

Our mothers warned us
they were dangerous.
How could those
brown-nosed pets
lead us into trouble?

We stuck them out,
we stuck them into mouths
to quiet infants and men.

Now, when the shadows
in our night rooms
might be anything,
we hold onto them.

My Daughter the Thief

It started with
makeup, hose,
earrings—
little things
she thought
I wouldn't miss.

Don't look at me!
she said—
like I was losing
my mind.

Then one day
when I wasn't looking,
she took
my breasts,
my hips.

Now she sneaks
out at night
who knows where
in my best dress.

Here I am
lying in bed
and my dress
is dancing,
and my hips
are shaking,
and who knows
what kind

of intoxicated,
filthy mind
keeps pawing
my breasts.

New Tenants

Something broke through,
stomping our separate
mole-tunnels of sleep.

We stared at the ceiling,
trying to piece sound
to see. A man and a woman

stood over us like gods
hurling their curses down
for signs. With each crash

I thought of Mad Kate
caught in a circling storm,
her eyes rimmed white

like plates. Words fell
through in broken beads
we could not put together.

The man said what he said
with his hands. We had
to feel to see; we could

have been anybody. Like two
moons in the eye of a drunk,
love lay still, listening,

the way children steal
through a wall at night
to know their future.

To My Mistress

—for Kathleen Brehony

I have little sadness of my own:
an empty bowl, age in my bones,
or, when the door shuts you out
and time stalls, an uneasy heart.

Something's wrong. Or going wrong.
I sense it. Last night, my head
in your lap as you read or tried
to read, your stroking hand
lay—a stilled bird—on my back.

And today on the beach
where we play and are healed,
your mind was like a stick
hurled to the horizon. Not even
my best antics could reach you.

I stood on the wracked shore
of a hurricane's postscript and felt
a squall, far out, racing toward us.

Doubt

One week of cherry blossoms,
one perfect summer's day
in April and I'm a fool for faith.

The goose sits on her nest.
Seed by seed, blackbirds
take religion at the feeder.

The dove mounts the dove;
mid-air, the fly rides the fly.
From a sky dusted in pollen,

pines lay their green shadows
down upon the river.
If I throw off my rags

would I stand, weightless
at the land's end, ready
to cross over?

Where Is the House?

Where is the house that will hold them?
Not his house with its one room.
Love would keep bumping into itself.
Love would shrivel and bruise.

And the things in her house,
like cats who have adjusted to one mistress,
would grow uneasy. How could love live
in a house of sighing cushions?

It must be a third house, a house
for this third person, them.
But where will she go when she aches
in all her corners to loosen loneliness?

But where will he go when he longs
for the dance of the bones in the howling place?
O the love that would fall in on itself!
O the love that would fly apart!

Where is the house that can hold them?

IV

Pelicans

They are born
in the old man's
clothes they will die in.
They know hunger
is big and comes first.
If they could speak
they would tell us
of the integrity of being
many things at once.

Instead they show us
the grace in clumsiness,
how to make light
of what we carry,
how to keep
in a straight line
loosely connected
to those who travel
with us.

A Leaf's Primer

Begin
detaching yourself
in advance.
Unhook need,
let mineral love
sluice backwards
in your veins.
Form a scab, seal over
the imagined wound
while you wait
for the cold
which is surely coming
with its perfunctory kiss,
for the darkness
that floods its borders
at both ends.
Worn to a sigh,
when the wind
muscles you
and the tree
shakes you off
and you feel like you're dying,
you must let
the only world you know
go on
falling
inside you.

Cancer Ward Game

It's a game—something to kill time,
Death explains. The solarium is bathed in light
and Sister Margaret is watering the white flags.

When you get there, he says, then pauses
for suspense—*if you could be with anyone...?*
Their eyes roll up. They are rummaging for names.

Are we limited to those who are history,
the newcomer wants to know,
or can we take our favorites with us?

You some kind of pharaoh? says Abe.
From her turban, Mrs. Esposito pulls a hairless
chihuahua. *Pepe,* she croons and strokes her lap.

Before long, the sunlit parlor is crowded:
Elvis, Jesus, the Marx Brothers
mixing with their own beautiful dead.

Everyone is excited, talking at once. More arrive.
They are kissing and hugging, the rear doors
of their gowns flapping, *Come in! Come in!*

What We're All Doing

You are doing what we're all doing,
only faster, like a bullet train,

your body honing itself,
hairless as a swimmer's,

and yet your going seems to us
so gradual, vegetable-slow

we hardly notice we visit less
of you or that you sit big-

eyed above the cross-
bones of your arms and legs.

And although you are only
doing what we're all doing,

your cancer like a flower
speeding through the film

of its life to show us our future,
we are ashamed

of ourselves, our newsiness,
our too-healthy passions,

the elaborate wrapping
of our flesh.

How You Stopped
—in memory of Noel

You stopped writing poems.
You placed your poems
in a box bigger than your life
and sealed it shut.
You stopped cooking.
You stopped inviting friends in
for soup and bread.
When your friends wouldn't stop
dying, you stopped
up the big mouth
of your front door;
you stopped up your ears
against the too-big world
you climbed a fire escape
to be safe from. You stopped
answering the telephone.
You stopped cleaning.
You stopped believing
that this life you weren't living
would pass, could pass
like a bad flu or a bad season.
Your world stopped working;
you stopped working.
You moved into your bed.
You moved into your head.
Glass after glass, you drowned
hours, whole weeks,
fears, passions, dreams,
a mother, a son—all the ghosts,
living and dead,
you couldn't stop loving.

When even that stopped working,
you turned off the television,
you turned off the music,
you put out your cigarette.
But because you couldn't stop
the whole idea of life,
you watered your plants,
you fed and walked your dog Sam
before you stopped.

The Visit

There were two of them
as if what they carried
was too heavy for one.

They stood in the doorway,
dark blue uniforms
backed in light.

Their faces were not sad or happy.

They asked to come in.
They had something to tell her.

Was she alone?
Was there anyone they could call
to be with her?

They told her to sit down.

Together they pulled
from their mouths
the name of her daughter.

Together they placed
the unbearable weight
in her lap.

Sharing Grief

We pass it back and forth
through telephone wires.
We divide it
into boxes—
yours, mine.
We compare the forms it takes
in the foreign countries
inside us.
Each day it is different;
each day it is the same.
Together,
we plant rocks.
Together,
we throw out
the empty hooks
of interrogatives:
Why *her* and not another?
Why not *us*?
Why like *that*?
Not "Why," time teaches us,
but "Is." If death is
nothing
but the end
of the accident of living,
we must learn to let go
of the universe
spinning a hole in our palms.

Trigger Points

For years, in invisible sacks
I have carried these aching
knots in my shoulder, my back
like broken commandments.

Now twice a week I lie on a table
and give myself
to a stranger's hands.

Kneading, pummeling, pressing,
for an hour he works his magic.

The *good pain*, he calls it.
Like the sweet despair of bringing back
someone or something lost.

Red Bud

—planted in memory of my daughter Jessica

This third spring, a blush,
barely a tinge of pink,
poked from a thin branch.

I have known them
wild in the mountains,
the first splashes of color
in the blue woods.

Again this summer
the few leaves, bitten
by blight, singed by sun,
hang like sick hearts.

The Hole

—on the yortzeit of my daughter

After years of looking at death,
wanting to believe in the impossible
resurrection, I dug up the red bud.

Planted in memoriam, the little tree
never grew into its name.

Such a hole! Such a big hole
for the childish roots
sunk just beneath the surface,
a face afloat on the underside
of the mind's thin ice.

I Don't Go There Anymore

At first I couldn't go
a day without going.
I'd lie on the new grass.
I'd talk to the sky.

On special occasions
I'd bring flowers—
daisies, yellow roses.
I planted a garden
of rocks.

Later, when words
wouldn't come,
I'd weed the bed.
I wanted her
place neat, orderly.

Now on Granby Street
when my hands on the wheel
would turn to enter
(O the pull
of memory's undertow),
cowardice? weakness?
a survivor's instinct?
cry *No!*

The Door

—after René Magritte

You've shut the door.
The brass knob stays still.
There's a thin vent at the bottom
where a letter might be shoved through
but the floor is bare. Nothing disturbs
dustballs that sleep at the threshold.
And yet, shadows slip in and slip out
in their hooded robes as if the heavy door
were a turnstile, a wisp of curtain.
Their step is soundless. When they open
their mouths question marks fly out
like startled blackbirds that dissolve
in the distance. It has to mean something—
this inexorable coming and going
like the heavy traffic of your thoughts
that keep arriving from nowhere
and depart on the first train out.

The Life that Goes on without You

Some days are like cows
following each other's tails
into pasture. It's raining.
You linger in bed
leafing through a book
the way you undress
a head of cabbage.
When the clock's
hands clap at noon,
your clothes
lay themselves out
like admonishing friends.
What's the use, your mind says
as your body moves.
The cats are fed,
the laundry
washed and folded.
Strangers drop in
through a mail slot.
Somebody pays the bills.
Or doesn't. Somebody
steers the car that returns
with its perishable cargo.
Hunger fixes dinner.
Full of itself, the garbage
walks out of the house
and doesn't look back.
It's still raining
in your head.
Black rain now.
Biblical.
In the living room
from a wealth of channels,

you can enter
any life you choose.

Inventory of Losses

The egg cup
and warm waters
of my mother

The miracle of being
a daughter
and the sun

A place
where people are safe
from each other

The little genius
of myself

My first dog
(the miles he loved
swallowed him)

Being visible
in any room
my sister entered

My prayers
ringed
in the ear of God

My parents' shine

The armed borders
of my body

At twenty,
my father's name

Two babies
before they were born

A marriage
steeled
against the wolf's storm

My mother's dreams
for my future

Two daughters
to their own lives

Lovers who fled
the whirlpool
of my neediness

When she was twenty-two,
by accident,
my baby

The power of my sex
(one day I walked into a room
and then men I didn't know
didn't notice me)

The lure of the far and the strange

Teeth;
the musculature
of verbs

To a good man's heart
in a distant state,
my other daughter

The bucket to the well
of names and dates

After urgency pulls me
into a certain room,
the noun I need
and came looking for

At the Feeder

They take their share and share
the narrow ledge. With every land
or leave, the whole house spins.

Clouds keep going by, and trees,
and three pink and white lawn chairs
polite as merry-go-round horses.

There's plenty and room enough,
the world seems to say,
until a black cloak swoops in.

Hanging by his toes, flapping
to keep afloat, he hurls down
seed like expletives.

Then, like a child's tantrum
that soon wears itself out,
he lifts to the pine's upper branches.

The briefly scattered finches
reclaim the ledge. There's plenty
and room enough, they confirm,

knowing how things turn
and turn around.

The Lesson of the Egret

She has already eaten
and the tide is moving out,
rippling across her reflection.

Unmoved by what moves
under her—a pulled stream
of blue crabs and silver fish,

unmoved by what moves
above and around her—
a wheeling racket of crows,

she roots at the center
like a white tear in the cove,
a peephole to the infinite,

alone, but not lacking,
alone, beyond wanting,
the small planet of her head

ranged away from her body,
the needle of her bill pointing
to a world without compass.

Yo-yo

If God is energy,
I sit in God's hand.
I ride a thread of desire—
my own—and not my own.

Longing spins me out.
There's genius in moving.
In dips and arcs I thrill
to the latitudes of air.

Habit winds me home.
It is good to rest
in the ring of myself.
There's genius in stillness.

A Late Serenade at Laurel Wood

I am surrounded by song—
cricket song, leaf song
scratching the air.
For fifty-eight years
I have known that nervousness.
Always, we have been intimate.

I am surrounded by trees.
I have known the shade
of trees, their moth-
bitten black umbrellas
for fifty-eight years.
Long ago, we became intimate.

I am surrounded by twilight.
For fifty-eight years
I have known what it's like
to walk, step by blind step,
into the night.
Recently, we became intimate.

I am surrounded by stars.
I have known these promisers
who blink and fidget
from a cold distance
for fifty-eight years.
Only now, we are intimate.

I Am Grateful for This Day

I am grateful
to wake with the sun
pouring through my window,
creeping across my bed
as if to touch me.

I am grateful
for the maple tree in my window,
the new nubs
on its thin branches,
their promise of opening
finger by finger
in an early spring.

I am grateful
for the birds
I see by hearing
in the tree in my window.
To wake to their calling
is to wake to the soft alarm
of a hand on a brow or cheek
that whispers, *Now*.

I am grateful
to move
into a day that has no hands
to push me or pull me
in the expediency of
This to be done!
That to be done!

I am grateful
to carry

in the cupped hands of memory
throughout my day
one who takes me,
inside him, everywhere—
to the store,
to the office,
to the mirror
he looks into to shave.

I am grateful
for the clock's hands
as they part and sweep
across the minutes to meet
each hour in prayer.

Counting Blessings

I no longer feel the compulsion to iron.

I can have any color hair I want.

I can indulge in the comfort
of white cotton underwear.

I have a better chance to be taken
seriously by men.

Like a dress that made me happy
when it hung two sizes too big,
my skin has become commodious.

I have grown to appreciate
the steadfastness of sleep.
When did another come nightly
and hold on for eight hours?

Everything is still possible
in dreams.

I get to revisit those I only thought I knew
decades ago in books.

Reading glasses are cheap.

The body keeps on
reminding me we're together in this.
Each new ache is a recommitment of vows,
an implicit faithfulness.

I am grateful
for the wisdom of the bowels,
how they know what to keep
and what to throw away.

I still have most of my teeth.

Thanks to the dilating holes
in memory's pockets,
there is less to keep track of.

My Honda has memorized the way.

I am no longer driven
by hormones to ride
roller coasters and bumper cars.

No one is pushing me on stage.

I have traded the cliff's edge,
conflagrations of the heart, rapids
for what is still at the center:

the mind content in its hammock
to watch thoughts drift
and change shape like clouds.

There is no one left
to tell me how to behave.

Some places give discounts.

Birthday on Brokenback Mountain

—for Michael

Late morning with only
the woods for neighbors,
I sit naked on the porch
and watch the sun unfurl

your gift of sixty roses.
Petal by slow petal, they relax
as all around cicadas
empty and refill—their chirr

so constant the hours forget
to notice. Late August and already
a litter of yellow leaves
brightens the forest floor.

Through glass doors:
the camber of your hip,
the gentle rise and fall of your
shoulder in disheveled sheets.

I remember your gift
of lacy nothings, lovemaking
that saw the stars go blind
in gray light. I remember

when I was little
I knew my grandmother was born
in a full-body corset
and heavy, black lace-up shoes.

Her upper arms flapped
like laundry on a line. Now
my daughter carries a child
who will rename me.

Cornflower, phlox, ox-eyed daisy
plucked from a field guide—
Later we'll walk these woods
with the comfort that comes

from addressing a thing
by its name. *Jane*, I say out loud.
Jane. It feels good—
this wind washing over me,

the sun climbing my back,
easing the arguments of bone,
the proximity of you who turn
toward me even as you sleep.

Acknowledgments

I am grateful to the editors of the magazines and journals, in which some of these poems, several in earlier versions, first appeared:

Blackwater Review: "The Visit" and "Sharing Grief"
Cider Press Review: "Inheritance"
Connecticut Poetry Review: "Inventory of Losses"
Dominion Review: "Pelicans" and "Cancer Ward Game"
Ghent Magazine: "The Cormorant"
Hayden's Ferry Review: "The Moronic Ox: A Fable"
Hollins Critic: "The Parrot-Ox"
Jewish Women's Literary Annual: "Red Bud" and "The Hole"
Kalliope, A Journal of Women's Art: "At the End of Down" and
    "My Daughter the Thief"
Poetry Northwest: "Another Time" and "Six Ways to Hide"
Quarterly of Light Verse: "Dog Days"
Southern Poetry Review: "New Tenants" and "What We're All Doing"
Southern Review: "After I Became a Poet"
State Street Review: "The Age of Animals"
Virginia Writing: "Earley Farm Road" and "The Wait"

"My Daughter the Thief," "Halcyon," "Another Time," "The Visit," "Sharing Grief," "Red Bud," "The Hole," and "I Don't Go There Anymore" were part of a sequence of mother/daughter poems performed in *Winter Tales by Candle Light* at the Generic Theater in Norfolk, Virginia, in December 2005 and were included in a publication of that program. Thanks to Robert Arthur, director, for his support of my work over many years.

Heartfelt thanks to Richard Mathews at the University of Tampa Press who, along with Donald Morrill and Martha Serpas, believed in my manuscript and provided meticulous care and invaluable assistance in refining its final form.

I am indebted to the Virginia Center for the Creative Arts for a fellowship which enabled me to work on this manuscript; to W. D. Snodgrass, my first and best teacher; to Mary McCue, my sister in poetry, for her editorial wisdom and support; to Mary-Jean Kledzik, who encouraged me to submit this manuscript to contests; to my partner Michael Perkins, who inspired and provided feedback for many of these poems; and to my beloved daughter Hara, my most generous critic, who shared the tenor of this work.

About the Author

Jane Ellen Glasser is the winner of the 2005 Tampa Review Prize for Poetry. Her poems have appeared in numerous journals, including the *Hudson Review*, *Southern Review*, *Virginia Quarterly Review*, *Georgia Review*, *Poetry Northwest*, and *Hayden's Ferry Review*. She has garnered awards for individual poems from the Irene Leache Society, Puddingstone, and the Poetry Society of Virginia, and has been recognized for outstanding articles on teaching poetry that were featured in *Virginia English Bulletin* and *English Journal*. A first collection of her poetry, *Naming the Darkness*, with an introduction by Pulitzer Prize-winning poet W. D. Snodgrass, was published by Road Publishers. For much of her life she has been active as an advocate for poetry. In the past she reviewed poetry books for the *Virginian-Pilot*, edited poetry for the *Ghent Quarterly*, and later co-founded the nonprofit arts organization and journal *New Virginia Review*. In addition, she has given presentations and conducted workshops for the International Society of Poetry, Writing Project at the College of William & Mary, the Tidewater Writing Project at Old Dominion University, and Florida's First Coast Writer's Festival, to name a few. For several years she served as poet-in-the-schools and visiting poet throughout Virginia before assuming a sixteen-year position as English and creative writing teacher at Norview High School in Norfolk, Virginia.

About the Book

Light Persists is set in Goudy Old Style types originally designed by Frederic W. Goudy for American Type Founders in 1915. When Goudy became art director of the Lanston Monotype Company of Philadelphia in 1920, his font was redesigned for that company to include the option of long descenders for smaller sizes, a feature retained in the digital version used in this book from the Lanston Type Collection of P22 Type Foundry in Buffalo, New York. Goudy spoke of his font as "an innovation in type," and he was especially pleased with the italic, of which he wrote in *A Half-Century of Type Design and Typography, 1895-1945:* "Taking the Aldine italic as a starting point for my new font, I began my work, and succeeded in producing an original letter which, I believe, constituted the first distinctive italic in modern times." The dove ornament that appears on the title page and elsewhere is by Swedish typographer Torbjörn Olsson to accompany his Dove type. The book has been designed and typeset by Richard Mathews at the University of Tampa Press. It is printed on acid-free recycled text paper and bound in Brillianta cloth from Ecological Fibers in support of the Green Press Initiative by Thomson-Shore of Dexter, Michigan.

Poetry from the University of Tampa Press

Jenny Browne, *At Once*

Richard Chess, *Chair in the Desert*

Richard Chess, *Tekiah*

Jane Ellen Glasser, *Light Persists**

Kathleen Jesme, *Fire Eater*

Lance Larsen, *In All Their Animal Brilliance**

Julia B. Levine, *Ask**

Sarah Maclay, *Whore**

John Willis Menard, *Lays in Summer Lands*

Jordan Smith, *For Appearances**

Jordan Smith, *The Names of Things Are Leaving*

Lisa M. Steinman, *Carslaw's Sequences*

Marjorie Stelmach, *A History of Disappearance*

Richard Terrill, *Coming Late to Rachmaninoff*

Matt Yurdana, *Public Gestures*

* *Denotes winner of the Tampa Review Prize for Poetry*